Sonnets to Malkmus

Ellen Dillon

Published by Sad Press in Brighton

April 2019

ISBN 978-1-912802-27-2

Cover by JLW

Set in Goudy Old Style

Song, as you teach him, is not desire,
not the touting of some final achievement;
Song is Being. Easy for a god.

(Rilke, *Sonnets to Orpheus*)

This pattern's torn
& we're weaving

(Pavement, 'Frontwards')

Part 1

True singing is different kind of breath.
A breath around nothing. A sigh in a god. A wind.

(Rilke, *Sonnets to Orpheus*)

Elder Boxing

Made all   my best life decisions   high school
& I'm afraid to say that you're not one   them
looked all   those demons four-square   eyeballs
kept most   my marbles   traded   some   them
mixed   best &   worst   this cow-town
usurped   mansplainers & peddlers   bull
sang solo polyphony   cronies & magnons

sang solo polyphony   cronies & magnons
usurped   mansplainers & peddlers   bull
mixed   best &   worst   this cow-town
kept most   my marbles   traded   some   them
looked all   those demons four-square   eyeballs
& I'm afraid to say that you're not one   them
made all   my best life decisions   high school

Seasonal Infant

My eyes stick   all   shiny roses
arms hold   weight   this whole world
lips licked look less like bacon   somehow
knees slapped   a bodily lightbulb
mouth 'ohs' its surprise   concerned emoji face
uterus   there's no you   it or anyone
spleen ideally keeps black bile   balance

spleen ideally keeps black bile   balance
uterus   there's no you   it or anyone
mouth 'ohs' its surprise   concerned emoji face
knees slapped   a bodily lightbulb
lips licked look less like bacon   somehow
arms hold   weight   this whole world
my eyes stick   all   shiny roses

There & Everywhere

Most times   most things have a sorrowful ring
anytime you're here there's shiny new sound
last time last time is the best time I spent
kale & spaghetti sound grosser than pie
most grocers lie   superfood soup
understand that it's not always easy to green
stand   your word but   sky

stand   your word but   sky
understand that it's not always easy to green
most grocers lie   superfood   soup
kale & spaghetti sound   grosser than pie
last time last time is the best time   I spent
anytime you're here   there's shiny new sound
most times   most things have a sorrowful ring

Stained

Moulded these crises
& held them hanging?
Loved too slightly
kept time-lines dangling
made bad connections
uncut their reelings
severed filaments

severed filaments
uncut their reelings
made bad connections,
kept time-lines dangling
loved too slightly
& held them hanging?
moulded these crises

Trig

More foreign   day   (line   to check   view)
a sneak peek   (they've opened   jam)
looks just like today   (I've got a message   you)
kicking   loose ones   (include a slip or two)
mix planet   a plate (tour city   a tram)
underscore   basic (connectedness   things)
seek   links (sausage: duck, venison or lamb)

seek   links (sausage: duck, venison or lamb)
underscore   basic   (connectedness   things)
mix planet   a plate (tour city   a tram)
kicking   loose ones   (include a slip or two)
looks just like today   (I've got a message   you)
a sneak peek   (they've opened   jam)
more foreign   day (line   to check   view)

Mouth a Dessert

Massage   oil & higher reasoning
& id is all we have   so wait
lament   better days gone dusting
keep souvenirs   creeping mould
maintain a casual listening stance
understand but don't fake soul
stand sidelong   giving nothing credence

stand sidelong   giving nothing credence
understand but don't fake soul
maintain a casual listening stance
keep souvenirs   creeping mould
lament   better days gone dusting
& id is all we have   so wait
massage   oil & higher reasoning

Sing Shot

My hands shook   down & out
all hands needed   this shot
loose hands find idle work
keep your hands where they can see
make a good hand   it
underhanded overheard
sleep   one hand wide open

sleep   one hand wide open
underhanded overheard
make a good hand   it
keep your hands where they can see
loose hands find idle work
all hands needed   this shot
my hands shook   down & out

Kid Kit

Make it count   quiet   sound-booth
as both   us smother a groan
leaving time to be marked   a rest or a pause
keeping   beats &   company bad
mixing long lines   short ones   texture
using   all   four-letter words
silent kid   don't lose your graceful tone

silent kid   don't lose your graceful tone
using   all   four-letter words
mixing long lines   short ones   texture
keeping   beats &   company bad
leaving time to be marked   a rest or a pause
as both   us smother a groan
make it count   quiet   sound-booth

Sounds Gold Pony Boy

Make another run   it
& keep my advent   yourself
lash a limelight-time   lilacs
kin & friends will know us best
mingle nuts   grapes & cheeses
undersell overwrought-iron resolve
solve   x   fraught equations

solve   x   fraught equations
undersell overwrought-iron resolve
mingle nuts   grapes & cheeses
kin & friends will know us best
lash a limelight-time   lilacs
& keep my advent   yourself
make another run   it

Breath Stopping

Make me a cake   to have & to eat

age me a steak   hanging & time

leave me alone strike   alone

keep   them   if you candle

melt all their brains   yr song

use all those puddles   evil

send 'em a wire   give 'em my best

send 'em a wire   give 'em my best

use all those puddles   evil

melt all their brains   yr song

keep   them   if you candle

leave me alone strike   alone

age me a steak with hanging & time

make me a cake   to have & to eat

Later Elevator

More than one way to stage a cat-skinning
anyone who's seen a nine-tailed one knows
later when we sift   ashes   glass beads
Klimt's leprous nudes will mouth shiny roses
Mary   sorrows will join us   plotting
undermining   wielder   pens   his task
so many fortresses & ways to attack

so many fortresses & ways to attack
undermining   wielder   pens   his task
Mary   sorrows will join us   plotting
Klimt's leprous nudes will mouth shiny roses
later when we sift   ashes   glass beads
anyone who's seen a nine-tailed one knows
more than one way to stage a cat-skinning

Rattled

Maybe it's penguins   players   sin-bins
always give extra   guitarists lose plectra
leave your lungs hurting   tucking my shirt
kabuki-white make-up   could use a shake-up
meet me   midnight   fist-fight
under or   this dog's not called Rover
several free-riders are buying hang-gliders

several free-riders are buying hang-gliders
under or   this dog's not called Rover
meet me   midnight   fist-fight
kabuki-white make-up   could use a shake-up
leave your lungs hurting   tucking my shirt
always give extra   guitarists lose plectra:
maybe it's penguins   players   sin-bins

G & Tea

Milk & cookies   Termonfecin
anchovy pizza   Cefalu
large cheeseburger meal   coke   Cork
kebab plate   fries & beer   Nice
merlot & tears   Sausalito
udon soup   pickles   London
spritzer   ice   New York   city

spritzer   ice   New York   city
udon soup   pickles   London
merlot & tears   Sausalito
kebab plate   fries & beer   Nice
large cheeseburger meal   coke   Cork
anchovy pizza   Cefalu
milk & cookies   Termonfecin

Arm a Dillo

Mash them a ceramic bowl
arrange it so they all have room
lay a bed scattered foliage
keep it   your best friend's arm
muss edges to make it real-like
undo links prior forms
save scraps other projects

save scraps other projects
undo links prior forms
muss edges to make it real-like
keep it   your best friend's arm
lay a bed scattered foliage
arrange it so they all have room
mash them a ceramic bowl

Ground

Magician   flesh   cleaving organs   splicing veins
&   parking lot   is   sedan he bought
life gives you lemonade   think   lives you saved
keep queasy souvenirs   toothy cysts   jars
make each incision count   let indecisions mount
use   summer break to shock yourself awake
steal   life   pay him back some other time

steal   life   pay him back some other time
use   summer break to shock yourself awake
make each incision count   let indecisions mount
keep queasy souvenirs   toothy cysts   jars
life gives you lemonade   think   lives you saved
&   parking lot   is   sedan he bought
magician   flesh   cleaving organs   splicing veins

Generation

Map   a world   boffins & changelings
anyone oblong & odd-shaped could name
look   people so tall   you
keep their eyes peeled when they talk   you
measure their hand-spans   pinkie   thumb
upend their hairpins & use them   fun
severing cities   sea   you next Tuesday

severing cities   sea   you next Tuesday
upend their hairpins & use them   fun
measure their hand-spans   pinkie   thumb
keep their eyes peeled when they talk   you
look   people so tall   you
anyone oblong & odd-shaped could name
map   a world   boffins & changelings

Lane Shade

Might all   this come crashing earthwards
& take us   richer plains
leave territories   twilight snipers
keep them occupied   daisy-chains
most can't yet see we're orbiting nothing
unfurling rubber gas-filled dreams
soon you're being told to recognize your heirs

soon you're being told to recognize your heirs
unfurling rubber gas-filled dreams
most can't yet see   we're orbiting nothing
keep them occupied   daisy-chains
leave territories   twilight snipers
& take us   richer plains
might all   this come crashing earthwards

Slow Types

Mate   I'm no funambulist I am only fun   I
amigos   eat no oranges   orange you all glad   I
lady   I am no Futurist   I'm my only critic   I
kinsmen   I have no ink-pen   I blot freehand   I
messieurs I am no Dutchman   my knickerbockers lie   I
uncles   I have ulcers or possibly carbuncles   I
sisters   I need assistance   nit-combing & seeing   I

sisters   I need assistance   nit-combing & seeing   I
uncles   I have ulcers or possibly carbuncles   I
messieurs I am no Dutchman   my knickerbockers lie   I
kinsmen   I have no ink-pen   I blot freehand   I
lady   I am no Futurist   I'm my only critic   I
amigos   I eat no oranges   orange you all glad   I
mate   I'm no funambulist I am only fun   I

Arranged

Make another way   & walk it   it ends
& maybe be that way   tracking cover   you go
leave   dust behind   &   rayon & polythene
keep   visor   &   ducks   screen
mute   laughter track   to provide your hollow own
u better walk   & leave   angles   shill
step   solid air   coyotes never really fall

step   solid air   coyotes never really fall
u better walk   & leave   angles   shill
mute   laughter track   to provide your hollow own
keep   visor   &   ducks   screen
leave   dust behind &   rayon & polythene
& maybe be that way   tracking cover   you go
make another way   & walk it   it ends

Chronically Underused

Make a batch   jet   torch
alter right   always wrong
let us breathe   not   press
keeping lungs   fast compressed
mix our blood just   tip
underuse sponsorship
steal a way   their stores

steal a way   their stores
underuse sponsorship
mix our blood just   tip
keeping lungs   fast compressed
let us breathe not   press
alter right   always wrong
make a batch   jet   torch

Harness

Minds   wide open truly
& madly drawn to mend
lightly twisting   hair   fingers
kiwis don't fling   those baking things
many   smooth & splice   pile
until they jingle   dangle & suspend
so judgement comes incrementally

so judgement comes incrementally
until they jingle   dangle & suspend
many   smooth & splice   pile
kiwis don't fling   those baking things
lightly twisting   hair   fingers
& madly drawn to mend
minds   wide open truly

Spit Danger

Make a better anger
& occupy a street
like a bitter stranger
keep minutes when we meet
meld   another angle
understand your poise
scan your marks   & Engels

scan your marks   & Engels
understand your poise
meld   another angle
keep minutes when we meet
like a bitter stranger
& occupy a street
make a better anger

Major O'Toole

Monetize a proper noun
angle   ringside seats
leverage your ball   grass
knee a stranger   groin
mandate anything at all
umbrage all   shade you can
steel yourself   pushing back

steel yourself   pushing back
umbrage all   shade   you can
mandate anything   all
knee a stranger   groin
leverage your ball   grass
angle   ringside seats
monetize   a proper noun

Spoke   Saw   Remembrance

Medley your songs   a club sandwich   sound
any spare bangers can be cut   outros
line   tools & try to find   sharp one
keep out-takes to put   when times are leaner
meld ending & beginning to make   best song
unpick   chords that tangled themselves   knots
someday develop   coast & sell   air

someday develop   coast & sell   air
unpick   chords that tangled themselves   knots
meld ending & beginning to make   best song
keep out-takes to put   when times are leaner
line   tools & try to find   sharp one
any spare bangers can be cut   outros
medley your songs   a club sandwich   sound

Space Vaguely

Made a sandwich to cure world hunger
a moment I could learn to love
left   toilet-seat   standby
kept score   a fallen dove
messed   connection   so much anger
unleashed   service   keeping   peace
some pieces got   way   a straight edge

some pieces got   way   a straight edge
unleashed   service   keeping   peace
messed   connection   so much anger
kept score   a fallen dove
left   toilet-seat   standby
a moment I could learn to love
made a sandwich   to cure world hunger

Son Cold

Meredith   you never looked like either
a sheen   A to be to see me fly
like a spindly Montgolfier brother
knobbly   sunset's ether wobble
made us muss our hair & learn   to cry
underneath   iridescent lining
sometimes it feels like   world's stuffed   feathers

sometimes it feels like   world's stuffed   feathers
underneath   iridescent lining
made us muss our hair & learn   to cry
knobbly   sunset's ether wobble
like a spindly Montgolfier brother
a sheen   A to be to see me fly
Meredith, you never looked like either

Part 2

Silent friend of many distances, feel
how your breath still multiplies all space.

(Rilke, *Sonnets to Orpheus*)

Seat Watered

Shade   county court
taking   a slack brief
everyone loves Chesapeakes
partly   retrieving
hiding   long grass
edging   water
never finding trouble there

Made all   my best life decisions   high school
arms hold   weight   this whole world
last time   last time is the best time I spent
kept time-lines dangling
mix planet   a plate (tour city   a tram)
understand but don't fake soul
sleep   one hand wide open

Midnight Animals

Starlings swerve   shattered kerb
to keep you   stoplights
every look tells more than   scowl
printed signs safeguard sandwiches & wine
hens peck, not scolding   scrabbling   seeds
earth clumps   churned   worms   worms clump
night falls   foxes scatter   owls dip   light stops

Make it count   quiet   sound-booth
& keep my advent   yourself
leave me alone   strike   alone
Klimt's leprous nudes will mouth shiny roses
meet me   midnight   fist-fight
udon soup   pickles   London
save   scraps   other projects

Saint Freezer

Squirrels   London found to have leprosy
tighten their clutch   a branch we must saw
except   earth &   mountains
prevent their fall   they'll catch us all
hanging   a wingtip   a tendril or a claw
every glitching twig-clutcher   rattled   their
need   needs   stall   we just saw   not fall

Magician   flesh cleaving organs   splicing veins
anyone oblong & odd-shaped could name
leave territories   twilight snipers
kinsmen   I have no ink-pen   I blot freehand   I
mute the laughter track   to provide your hollow own
underuse sponsorship
so judgement comes incrementally

Death Ramp

Stalled climactically   weather
time folds & holds us
elegantly tapered fingers stroke
piece it together
hands neglect to rummage where they should
endlessly smoothing
nerve ends   microfibre's fizzy static

Make a better anger
angle   ringside seats
line   tools & try to find   sharp one
kept score   a fallen dove
made us muss our hair & learn to cry
usurped   mansplainers & peddlers   bull
spleen ideally keeps black bile   balance

Whitechurch

Stack   books
tenth   May
everybody
pot   gold
half a line
endless night
ninth & Hennepin

Most times   most things have a sorrowful ring
& held them hanging?
looks just like today (I've got a message   you)
keep souvenirs   creeping mould
make a good hand   it
using   all   four-letter words
solve   x   fraught equations

Mirror Bonus

Slayer bells   warbling doves   anemones slow
tourniquets   runaways glazing hotel soap
everyone loves restitution   abstractly owe
pop   rec room little man   snow
hold   a better lace   a dazzling bow
easy come   easy come   easy come   go
nowhere we never think yet somehow we know

Make me a cake   to have & to eat
anyone who's seen a nine-tailed one knows
leave your lungs hurting tucking my shirt
kebab plate   fries & beer   Nice
muss   edges to make it real-like
use   summer break to shock yourself awake
severing cities   sea   you next Tuesday

Trash Emotion

Salty where we meet
tumbling your frame
emptying that tide
pining   claim
hankering   you
even though you're here
never going to stray

Might all   this come crashing earthwards
amigos   I eat no oranges   orange you all glad I
leave   dust behind   &   rayon & polythene
keeping lungs   fast compressed
many smooth & splice   pile
understand your poise
steel yourself   pushing back

Bob's Jacket

Stay   Christmas Day
taking umbrage when it's offered
easy to see   looking
pretty   a thread bear-skin
hunt something to burrow
emerald & lilac tinted
neckerchiefs make space to breathe

Medley your songs   a club sandwich   sound
a moment I could learn to love
like a spindly Montgolfier   brother
kept most   my marbles traded   some   them
mouth 'ohs' its surprise (concerned emoji face
understand that it's not always easy) to green
severed filaments

Clarence Skiboots

Snakes age   finding ways not to be footwear
the sin taxi encodes your fare take your belongings when you   go
elders box us   circus-ring locution
prime location-specific prepositions leave us hanging   mid-   air
hors d'oeuvres   sound that don't fill   that gap
either here or there & rattled   ordered words
neither this nor that & ordered   word rattles

More foreign   day   (line   to check   view)
& id is all we have   so wait
loose hands   find idle work
keeping   beats &   company bad
mingle nuts   grapes & cheeses
use all those puddles evil
so many fortresses & ways to attack

Rot Pencils

Second thoughts   you & first regrets
turn   fidgeting & wandering eyes
everybody had a second love
pleating chronology you had yours first
handling implications like they're paper planes
entangling anglepoises to shed complex light
near tangled paper questions poised   cut or flight

Maybe it's penguins   players   sin-bins
anchovy pizza   Cefalu
lay a bed   scattered foliage
keep queasy souvenirs   toothy cysts   jars
measure their hand-spans   pinkie   thumb
unfurling rubber gas-filled dreams
sisters I need assistance   nit-combing & seeing   I

Boy Paint Post

Self-dying hair I concocted   a
tincture   rainbows   blinkers
each colour could fashion a timer
post-paint boy   your art
hair-sculpture seems like a bristling beginning
everything tangible moves   your
never-still fingers   zinging   shade

Make another way   & walk it   it ends
alter right   always wrong
lightly twisting hair   fingers
keep minutes when we meet
mandate anything   all
unpick   chords that tangled themselves   knots
some pieces got   way   a straight edge

Dog   Jen S

Silence climbs   our ears   end
the stains   your outro still clinging
emptying itself   vacant straits
plenty   time to quell that pretender
he's   Ess-Dog   Sean if you wish
enough to let us think   jangling
not all   dire threads end   song

Meredith you never looked like either
& I'm afraid to say that you're not one   them
lips licked look less like bacon   somehow
kale & spaghetti sound grosser than pie
made bad connections
underscore   basic   (connectedness   things)
stand sidelong   giving nothing credence

Real Agers

Stacking odds can lead
tumbling chance   boulders rolling
evenly   this great old
plain   ours   they stop
heaps   inevitable whose
elevation is so high we can
never climb to see   other side

My hands shook   down & out
as both   us smother a groan
lash a limelight-time   lilacs
keep   them   if you candle
Mary   sorrows will join us   plotting
under or   this dog's not called Rover
spritzer   ice   New York   city

Love   Stick-figures

Someone is doing
things   fall apart
every time
process grins   a
halt   a scrub   words
everyone does understand one
no one is done

Mash them   a ceramic bowl
&   parking lot   is   sedan he bought
look   people so tall   you
keep them occupied   daisy-chains
messieurs   I am no Dutchman   my knickerbockers lie I
u better walk away   & leave   angles   shill
steal away   their stores

Shoeless　Joe

Spare me your contrarian thaw
take a shine　　someone's flaws　　once
elevate them　　a countermeasure feature
pulsed　　　　　　springs　meltwater
humming　　muffled speech-bubbles;
extreme measures only value either end
nothing　　middle registers　　no noun counts

Minds wide open truly
& occupy a street
leverage your ball　　grass
keep out-takes to put　　when times are leaner
messed　　connection　　so much anger
underneath　　iridescent lining
sang solo polyphony　　cronies & magnons

Spice & Orientation

Seeing   corner isn't easy;
taking   this windswept afternoon
eyes swivel   they meet   vanishing
point & bend no further no sweeping
hanging   a moon-sliver. There'd be no
eyeballs left   Gaza or anywhere   if we bowled
nutmeg strikes   curved horizon

My eyes stick   all   shiny roses
anytime you're here there's shiny new sound
loved too slightly
kicking   loose ones   (include a slip or two)
maintain a casual listening stance
underhanded overheard
silent kid   don't lose your graceful tone

Unreal Motion Trash

Stepping   cliff   speed
this acme jetpack will sputter
easy said but less often done
plumbing depths   plummeting deaths
hang suspended   a twig like
every rag- thread-   & garbage-wig birds
nest cresting a branch to hold still

Make another run   it
age me a steak   hanging & time
later when we sift   ashes   glass beads
kabuki-white make-up   could use a shake-up
merlot & tears   Sausalito
undo   links   prior forms
steal   life   pay him back some other time

Churching Wyatt

Spelling   light pours   us
till our sight overflows & shadows
everything   its backing   splodges
plus   truth   I only poured you
half   light to show   dark lining
edging vision's flower & binding us
nucleus is family   dazed   spelled & bound.

Map   a world   boffins & changelings
& take us   richer plains
lady   I am no Futurist   I'm my only critic I
keep   visor   &   ducks   screen
mix our blood   just   tip
until they jingle   dangle & suspend
scan your marks   & Engels

50

Willie Hopscotch

Sometimes it seems like   world
takes a break   being seen
everyone slipping   to find
playmates   keen   to   let   them   know
he was a mark not a killer
even if he always brought   end
never one   his marked unworldly friends

Monetize a proper noun
any spare bangers can be cut   outros
left   toilet-seat   standby
knobbly   sunset's ether wobble
mixed   best &   worst   this cow-town
uterus   there's no you   it or anyone
stand   your word   but   sky

Elmo

Stalk your street like a crackling god
tingling   red fuzz static   tactile
energy   tickling   fire   rub
palm-pads   fur-fronds'
haptic garden   face-blind
elusive like consume to acquire
niceties   can be lacquered   afterwards

Moulded these crises
a sneak peek   (they've opened   jam)
lament   better days gone dusting
keep your hands where they can see
mixing long lines   short ones   texture
undersell overwrought-iron resolve
send 'em a wire   give 'em my best

Delmo

Should you need to cast a spell
take this skein   wonderweb
extend it   a wrist-flick   double
plait it mid-air a quick twitch
hemming   sound   hawing & filling
even   words fall still your
nonstop grin

More than one way to stage a cat-skinning
always give extra   guitarists lose plectra
large cheeseburger meal   coke   Cork
keep it   your best friend's arm
make each incision count   let indecisions mount
upend their hairpins & use them   fun
soon you're being told to recognize your heirs

Garden

So you got some curve appeal
tangerine skies embrace   hills' curves
extending our sightline   four dimensions
peeling your eyeballs back   crossed lines hurt
hydrangea's bunched folds hold all space & time
entwined   winter their empty heads will eye   snow
nodding   crunching drifts   piled dense crystals

Mate   I'm no funambulist   I am only fun I
& maybe be that way   tracking cover   you go
let us breathe   not   press
kiwis don't fling those baking things
meld another angle
umbrage all   shade you can
someday develop   coast & sell   air

Baltimore or Less

Stopping hearts   mid-beat   a torn scream
the panic is leaking   every clear pore
each stretch   skin oozing frantic miasma.
Please don't take this   wrong way but you were
helped   this world   bloody coiling things
exploded rings   viscera recoiled us   adrenalized
nesting   entrails   we pulled you clear & porous   .

Made a sandwich to cure world hunger
a sheen   A to be to see me fly
looked all   those demons four-square   eyeballs
knees slapped   a bodily lightbulb
most grocers lie   superfood soup
uncut their reelings
seek   links (sausage: duck, venison or lamb)

Red Share

Since none   us is new
to this time & place
everything we tried to lose
permeates   sectioned layers
holding us still. Born too slippy
etched too deep   crawl   what
never yields to sleep or permanence.

Massage   oil & higher reasoning
all hands needed   this shot
leaving time to be marked   a rest or a pause
kin & friends will know us best
melt all their brains   yr song
undermining   wielder   pens   his task
several free-riders are buying hang-gliders

A Trial

Shrugging   congealed regrets I see
that none   this was planned yet most sticks
even   doubt skirts our knees & rises.
People look great when they shave   don't they?
Hanging   vice-like   that   we can go
entertaining fancies   doing everything otherwise
not needing   really   to go   that first gret.

Milk & cookies   Termonfecin
arrange it so they all have room
life gives you lemonade   think   lives you saved
keep their eyes peeled when they talk   you
most can't yet see we're orbiting nothing
uncles I have ulcers   or possibly carbuncles I
step   solid air   coyotes never really fall

Dragonfly

School's   forever   fish-boy
time to learn water & shoal-thinking
each spurious link   water & air
Piscean life-skills will bloom & swerve
high school principal   show & tell.
Earth repels all   us   preferring   stolid
nebulous   vaporous   part-porous us

Make a batch   jet   torch
& madly drawn to mend
like a bitter stranger
knee a stranger   groin
meld ending & beginning to make   best song
unleashed   service   keeping   peace
sometimes it feels like   world's stuffed   feathers

Street Independence

Somebody lurks faintly
throwing love instead   shade
elbows braced   concentration
point contritely both ways
here is where it ends   not there
everybody hurts
no-one can work   where

Meredith   you never looked like either
a moment I could learn to love
line up   tools & try to find   sharp one
knee a stranger   groin
meld another angle
until they jingle   dangle & suspend
steal a way   their stores

Flake Away

Sieving gravel   nuggets
turned us grungy   inside-out
eating chalk-dust made us drier
planting lines   you to find
hid us   ourselves a while
edged us close   you   staging
non-stop banter   heart supplanter

Make a batch   jet   torch
& maybe be that way   tracking cover   you go
lady   I am no Futurist   I'm my only critic   I
keep them occupied   daisy-chains
measure their hand-spans   pinkie   thumb
use   summer break to shock yourself awake
save   scraps   other projects

Sheets

Stutters me   head   toe
turns me like a phrase
evokes me   a code word
parses me   syntax trees
hums me   a sequenced ear-worm
exclaims me   derision
notes me   margins.

Mash them   a ceramic bowl
anchovy pizza   Cefalu
leave your lungs hurting   tucking my shirt
Klimt's leprous nudes will mouth shiny roses
melt all their brains   yr song
undersell overwrought-iron resolve
silent kid   don't lose your graceful tone

Acknowledgements

Selections from *Sonnets to Malkmus* have previously appeared in *Zarf* and the *Free Poetry Irish Anthology*. Thanks to Callie Gardner for accepting them for *Zarf*, and to Martin Corless-Smith for the opportunity to edit the anthology. The sequence was conceived in response to an invitation from Sam Solomon to read at the Sussex Poetry Festival in 2017 so huge thanks to Sam and all at Sussex.